Love Always, Rose

ROSE WILCOX SLIEMERS

WESTBOW
PRESS®
A DIVISION OF THOMAS NELSON
& ZONDERVAN

WestBow Press books may be ordered through booksellers or by contacting:

WestBow Press
A Division of Thomas Nelson & Zondervan
1663 Liberty Drive
Bloomington, IN 47403
www.westbowpress.com
1 (866) 928-1240

ISBN: 978-1-9736-8051-2 (sc)
ISBN: 978-1-9736-8053-6 (hc)
ISBN: 978-1-9736-8052-9 (e)

Library of Congress Control Number: 2019919634

Print information available on the last page.

WestBow Press rev. date: 12/10/2019

A Woman's World

W – Wife
O – Organizer
M – Mother
A – Author/poet
N – Nurse

Jack

You are my rock;
you keep me strong
and give me hope
when days are long.

My heart is full;
thank God above.
He has given us
unending love.

You give me strength
when I am weak;
you make me smile
when things look bleak.

At times, we grow weary
while running this race,
but God has given us amazing grace.

We've worked hard to answer God's call,
and with our love, we have it all!

Love always, Rose

Our Children

Our children are our gifts
of life's eternal love.
We thank you, Lord, for giving us
these treasures from above.

Such joy they bring
to us each day
in all they do and all they say,
with God to help along the way.

Those growing years have long since passed;
we're so proud of all they've done.
We've tried to raise our children
as Mary and Joseph did their Son.

Love always,
Mom and Dad

Our Grandchildren

Our lives have been blessed
with the most precious things:
our children and grandchildren,
all angels without wings.

They bring us love and laughter
and fill our hearts with pride,
these precious gifts from heaven
with God to help and guide.

Love always,
Grandma Rose and Grandpa Jack

A Penny from Heaven

I was sitting quietly in church and feeling really blue,
remembering loved ones suddenly gone.
I didn't have a clue
that God was sitting next to me,
surrounding me with love,
when my angel dropped a penny
straight from heaven up above.
Right next to me, I saw it
beside me in the pew—
this penny sent from heaven
all bright and shiny and new.
It was from my heavenly angel
trying to cheer me from above
to mend my aching heart
with her tender, gentle love.
So many tears have fallen;
it's just so hard to accept
why God would take our loved ones—
I've tried so hard, and yet.
Please help me understand, Lord;
please help me find release.
Please dry my tears, relieve my heart,
and send us all your gentle peace.

Promoted to Nurse

Our story begins on the fourth of July.
Probies we were, so scared and so shy.
With brave hearts, we entered the halls of doom
and filed slowly to our room.
All was silent for six weeks or more
as we studied till dawn behind the closed door.
Then, at last, came our uniforms, all shiny and white;
on duty we'd go in another fortnight.
Our day's work finished, so tired, so dead,
we quickly made ready to go to bed.
Six weeks are now gone; our caps are here.
With a yawn and a sigh, we breathe a cheer.
Working morning, noon, and night
all tired and worn—oh, what a sight.
The next few years will quickly pass;
then finally, at last,
we'll once again take our stand,
file slowly hand in hand.
We'll gladly accept our diplomas with pride,
being thankful at last—it's the end of the ride.

Sleep Softly Now

So quickly did the summer pass,
I didn't see it go.
T'was quite a time for fun and games,
and oh, I miss it so.
The wind appeared, and with the gale,
the trees began to sway;
the leaves held tight with all their might
but slowly slipped away.
This sudden surge of nakedness
added to their woe;
their branches bowed in true distress
and waited for the snow.
Softly it came and gently fell,
caressing every bough,
a blanket white to cover them
and keep them safe for now
until the spring returns again
with warmth and gentleness.
Sleep softly, now, you stately trees;
enjoy a peaceful rest.

My Hometown

I took a walk through my hometown
and walked around the square.
I passed some stores so very new
and began to wonder where
the ice cream parlor could have gone.
I know it stood right there.

I took a stroll down memory lane,
and how my heart did swell.
I passed the corner five and dime
and thought of my best pal
and of the happy bygone days that
I remember well.

I ventured a wee bit farther
to see what I could see.
I turned around and looked again
and thought, *How can it be?*
So many things had changed somehow
and seemed so strange to me.

I walked past homes that I once knew,
seeking a friendly face,
then took a stroll down Old Main Street
but felt most out of place.
I looked at all the new people
and thought of time and space.

As I prepared to leave the scene,
something within me sighed,
for nothing seemed to be the same;
progress had found its stride.
My heart was filled with much sadness,
for part of me had died.

What Is Love?

It's being together always,
sharing hopes and dreams,
accepting the good as well as the bad,
both part of the scheme.

It's trusting and depending
on each other day and night,
giving encouragement when feeling down,
and knowing that it's right.

It's arguing and disagreeing
when something seems to go wrong—
but only a fight that's fairly fought
can strengthen and make love strong.

It's the softness of a gentle cloud
with a slow-moving ship sailing through.
Walking together, hand in hand,
in the breeze by the ocean blue.

It's all the little, thoughtful things
that both of us must do
just as a part of living
to show that love is true.

When Death Stalks

I grow so weary, day by day;
I need help to find the way.
My eyes grow dim, my spirits weak;
sweet release is what I seek.
Into the dark of night he came;
caressingly, he called my name.
I tried so hard to see his face;
my weary body couldn't meet the pace.
I prayed for freedom and relief;
I saw him come, and like a thief,
he tried to steal my soul away
yet feared the brightness of the day.
Who's to say and who's to know
when the time is set to go?
Only God has the final say
to take my soul and spirit away.
Please, Lord, if you find it in your heart,
grant my release, so I may depart
and leave behind my pain and sorrow,
so I can prepare for the great tomorrow.

Growing Old

I never stopped to think before
what growing old would mean.
Somehow, that seemed so far away,
beyond my wildest dreams.

Then one day—last week, in fact—
while I was combing my hair,
I suddenly spied that strand of gray
and could only stop and stare.

Good heavens, I thought, *I'm turning gray.*
I blinked and rubbed my eyes.
I tried real hard to brush it away;
I nearly thought I'd die!

Running blindly to the door—
on the way, I grabbed my sweater—
when I heard a voice say, "Hold on, girl.
You're not getting old, just better."

I stopped short and stood up straight;
suddenly I felt real good.
I remembered my mother always said
gray was a badge of womanhood.

So I stood up tall and squared my shoulders.
I felt an inner pride,
for I knew the badges that mothers earn
were not the kind to hide.

In the Beginning

When the creator of all humankind
set forth his infinite plan,
he knew he needed a helpmate
to aide and assist man.
So he worked both day and night
to find the perfect one.
For this man, Adam, was the finest,
in the image of his Son.
After much deliberation,
he made a counterpart
fashioned from Adam's rib
but with a much larger heart.
He gave his new creation strength
unsurpassed by any man.
It seemed he anticipated this all
as part of the master plan.
And then he smiled contentedly,
stepped back to have a view—
the perfect man and woman
all so fresh and new.
He then helped them on their way
by placing them in paradise.
But like always happens,
a dream can melt before your eyes.
Temptation seemed to rear its head.
How saddened he must have been
that after all his love and care,
humans gave in to sin.
The story does not end here, as all are now aware.
Humans were sent out on their own from the shelter with God's care.
And so, people must struggle, must work both day and night
to prove to God once again they're worthy of what had been their right.

God's Love

Share what little you may have
with someone who has less.
Then the angels will smile on you,
and God your life will bless.
I remember years ago,
when young and newly wed,
my husband gave a poor, small girl a dime.
I didn't stop to think; he was following the Lord's request:
"You give to me when you give
to the least of mine."
The years have quickly flown, and we've been truly blessed.
I remember that night years ago
when my husband shared what little we had,
and because of that, God's love he now does show.

Think of Me

If everything you do
doesn't go right,
if days seem long
and you dread the night
or darkness seems to dim the light,
think of me.
If life seems dull
or has lost its glow,
you feel depressed,
the teardrops flow,
you can't go on
because you're feeling so low,
think of me.
If you need a friend to listen,
someone who understands,
just to stop a while
or maybe hold your hand,
think, please think of me.

Company Room

For years, I longed
to have a spare room
to invite our guests to stay.
But each room was filled
with a sleeping child.
I told myself, *Someday!*

I mentally planned this dream house
included that extra spare room,
a sewing niche,
a sun porch—
in the kitchen, a matching broom.

The years seemed
to quickly fly.
The children left their cocoon
and went off their separate ways.
It happened all too soon.

I guess
I really didn't stop
to think or realize
that only when the children left
could my dream
materialize.

So now,
I have a company room—
but I find
I must confess,
the quiet that prevails the house
leaves me in great distress.

I Sometimes Question

I sometimes question
why things are
or why they have to be,
it's not that I doubt
God's wisdom,
I'm just unsure of me.
I know my inner feelings
sometimes guide
what I do and say,
and I just want
reassurance that
I won't be led astray.
So, God, watch me closely
day and night,
somehow guide my way.
Give me the courage to carry on
If I chance to stray.

The Night's Silence

Night falls,
and the sound of silence
is magnified
to the point of madness.
How I long
for your arms
to hold me.
My body aches
for the warmth of your embrace.
God, I miss you so.
I lie here alone
wondering where you could be
and if you
miss me as well.
Tomorrow,
as the sun softly
caresses your soft skin,
it will be me,
my love,
sending you my kisses.

An Angel In Disguise

The angels in the heavens
worked all through the night,
to fashion us a vision
all dressed in snowy white.
Her lips were fashioned
from the choicest wine;
the brightest stars made up her eyes.
Her hair evolved from the very
distant, darkest portion of the skies.
Her teeth were like pearls,
and her cheeks were red bright.
My, but they worked
right through the long night.
Finally, at last, the waiting was through,
on a clear, lovely morning
with the skies so blue.
They brought forth this vision,
all good and all sweet,
to give to the world for all mankind to meet.
Her radiant smile, her sparkling eyes,
she was indeed
an angel in disguise.
All helpful, all joyful,
always the first
to offer her services to those in need.
Saying, "don't worry, it won't get any worse."
A loan from the good Lord,
ah yes, indeed.
Never heeding her own desires; humanity always comes first.
This angel in white, so pure, so sweet, happens to be
our own little nurse.

Seek and You Will Find

I find as time has moved along,
dreams mellowed with the years.
For every lost hope on the way,
I've shed a million tears.
Still I falter and grow afraid,
there's so much left to do.
The future looks so bleak and gray,
who will help me … who?
Who will share my lonely path
offer a helping hand.
Suddenly a light shone thru the night
to help me understand,
that if I seek, so shall I find,
peace and love, above all hope.
And with his guidance also find
the tools with which to cope.

I'd Rather Be Home

I love the way your eyes follow me
across a crowded room.
I love the way you give me a quick wink
to reassure me,
you're not far away.
Funny, it gives me a feeling
or warmth and protectiveness,
both at the same time.
You know, I'd rather
be home with you,
alone, rather than in this
crowded room,
making small talk,
being sociable,
when
all I want
is to feel the safe security
of your arms around me.

Don't Try

Don't try to second-guess the Lord,
or try to figure why
he's calling me to visit him
in his castle in the sky.
Could be he's reassigned some tasks
and needs a helping hand,
to keep the angels on their course;
I'm sure he has a plan.
'Cause mama always used to say
don't ever question why.
Things happen differently than you planned,
won't do no good to cry.
For only God knows the reason
some folks live, some folks die,
and I like to think he needs me
in that castle in the sky.

The "Hotline"

We had a hotline to heaven
to see us through the day.
God was standing ever close
to help us on our way.
And, as we have always known,
when we place our trust in God,
He gives us courage, guides our way,
where first we feared to trod.

The Blizzard in Ohio

A strange feeling came over me
when I first got out of bed.
I looked around, the silence grew,
I knew it was a day to dread.
I took a cautious look outside,
the quiet seemed to wider spread.
No sound was heard, not a person stirred,
I wished I was back in bed.
The vicious wind whipped through the trees;
I could barely see the ground.
The chill in the air seemed to colder grow
and I knew we were snowbound!
All day, it raged, and the town stood still,
while the snow seemed to steadily fall.
We seemed suspended in time and place;
no one could hear our call.
A winter like we'd never seen;
the drifts were mountains high,
the country at a standstill,
with nothing passing by.
And yet, the snow was beautiful,
untouched, without a mar.
I think to make man more aware
we're governed by a Greater Power.

The Golden Years

Now is the time to savor, to cherish
the rushing, the struggle to survive.
Now is the forming of the memory
that strives to keep later years alive.

This day, with the changing of the season,
mold the dreams, later years expound.
This world and all the promises within it;
later memories recall and rebound.

All joys and sorrows are a part of life,
as later we recall the pain and tears.
Hold fast the precious memories,
for these truly are the golden years.

Nature Triumphs

The trash was scattered on the ground;
the garbage seemed to overflow.
Cans and bottles strewn around;
the pile of rubble seemed to grow.
A blight upon our city,
an eyesore to be sure;
no one made the effort
to find the answer or the cure.
But last week as I drove by;
I suddenly noticed a change.
The corner somehow seemed different,
even a little strange,
and then I knew the reason.
A spray of wildflowers growing free
had totally covered the rubble.
Only fresh blossoms could I see,
hiding the bottles and the trash.
The wildflowers stood proud,
smothering the garbage and the cans
with beautiful flowers—like a shroud.

Help Me Understand

The heartache and the pain they feel today;
words alone cannot describe in any way.
To lose a loved one so very young,
so hard to accept or believe.
My heart aches with the pain they must face.
My soul in sorrow does grieve.
Oh God, please help me understand;
I know there must be a reason.
To every happening on the earth;
there is a time, a season.
It's just that I find it hard to accept
the death of one so young.
He had so much vitality,
so many songs unsung.
Help me see the wisdom of your ways,
why such pain must be.
Then my doubting heart will rest;
understanding will set me free.

Believe in Me

I used to dream of perfect happiness
when I was young and unaware.
—Believe—
My heart kept saying,
Believe, and it will happen.
My imagination ran wild
as my yearnings grew stronger.
—Believe—
But dreams are not reality,
and life is not all perfect,
with no patches to mar the quilt of life,
and now I see,
it is not perfect happiness I long for;
instead, I only hope that you
believe—in me!

Please God

On days when I'm feeling unusually blue,
burdened with tasks, too many to do,
I look beyond the earth to the sky
to the floating clouds, so fluffy white.
My heart skips a beat as the wind passes by;
my soul makes ready for a midsummer's flight.
Oh, take me with you; let me climb aboard
to faraway places I long to see,
with dancing feet and a heart that sings.
Let me follow the star that is calling me.
Let me ride with the wind, sail over the clouds,
float through that limitless space,
leaving behind all my earthly cares.
Please, God, help me find such a place.

Ohio, My Home

I've seen the beauty of the mountains
and the sage brush on the plain.
The oceans of wheat, the silky corn,
fields of hay and grain.

The barren plains, the tumbleweed,
the vast expanse of skies.
The beauty of the painted desert;
a sunset glow that dies.

Great herds of cattle roaming free
on the topmost mountain range.
The oil wells with liquid gold,
so different and rather strange.

The antelope, the elk, the deer,
traveling free in the dawn of morn.
The scent of sage, so sharp and clear,
the breeze that's mountain born.

The wealth of Vegas, I'll not forget;
the money flowed like wine.
But despite the wonders that I've seen,
I find my heart does pine.

For the country roads, I know so well,
where there's grass that's emerald green.
The sky, bluer than the ocean's blue,
the trees, the tallest seen.

The air so fresh and clean and clear,
that no matter where I roam,
the peace I find in Ohio land
is the place that I'll call my home.

To Man

Man is a strange, unpretentious creature,
humble, subdued, a bit of the old sod.
One wrinkle in his best white shirt
brings out the devil in him, the clod.

He likes to be pampered, looked up to and loved,
his dinner served with a smile.
"Bring me a beer," you're sure to hear,
The TV blaring all the while.

Yes, man is a strange unpretentious creature
whose moods one cannot capture.
Who could guess that growl in the morning
might lead to an evening of rapture?

We can't live with them,
they're temperamental and blue.
Can't live without them;
oh, what can we do?

I can't write the end
to this pickle of a riddle;
although I'm not fickle,
I'm caught in the middle.

The Heart

The heart survives many things
life may have in store.
Sorrow, pain, mixed with joy
and much, much more.
A tiny babe's first fall brings tears.
His first step, joy to the heart.
Then off to school; can it be so soon
he had to part?
His first award brings pride and smiles;
an injury brings tears.
A first offense starts the trials
that are the formative years.
But the heart keeps on hoping
love will guide his way;
he's just a tiny little babe
who suddenly grew up one day.

Angel Unaware

Poor little babe,
sweet and innocent,
fresh and new,
from God heaven sent.
Trusting to fate
while struggling to live,
totally unaware.
No chance will they give.
Plans are forming
(no one ever asked him)
to end his life
before it begins.
Poor little babe,
alone, defenseless.
Why would anyone choose
to do something so senseless?
Can't they hear my plea?
I've a right to live.
It's my fate they're sealing.
Just one chance, can't you give?

Please, Mom, I'll be good.
I'll make you proud of me.
Just let me live!
Oh God, let me be!

Nurse's Prayer

As we awake each morn
and don our uniforms of white,
we dream of yesterdays gone by,
the lonesomeness of night.
We dream of all the happiness,
the love of long ago,
and pray that someday we will find
a life devoid of woe.
As we go about our duties,
sometimes happy, maybe sad,
we also dream of yesteryear
and the fun we always had.
We pray for happiness to come,
for joy to fill our heart,
and suddenly back to earth,
we tumble with a start.
If only it were possible
and all our dreams came true,
I'd wish my life on earth were filled
each endless day with you.
When my life on earth is over,
and our life begun above,
I'll thank the Lord, my darling,
that you had been my love.

Conflict

My husband gets so irate
when the cleaning has to wait.
While I pursue my special dreams
explore, shop, or scheme my schemes.
But I've learned, and this I know:
dreams may fade and lose their glow.
Time just moves so fast today,
it seems somehow to slip away.
So husband dear, I'm sorry,
as sorry as can be.
The dust will just have to wait;
it surely won't dissipate.
I must pursue my special dreams,
explore, shop, and scheme my schemes.
I have no time for dirt and grime;
I'll clean the house another time.

My Mom Was Different

Sue was different, so very special
in her own loving way,
so giving of her time and self;
I miss her more each day.
Many seek fame and fortune,
searching the world wide;
Mom found joy in simpler things,
like family by her side
(but she was different).
There are those who strive for praise,
seeking world acclaim.
Mom was happy and content
when friends and neighbors came.
(She was different.)
She gave us many memories;
she gave us love and hope,
but most of all she gave us strength
and faith with which to cope.
(Yes, she was different.)
She had her share of sorrow,
sadness, and despair.
But nothing could defeat her;
her faith was always there.
(Yes, she was different.)

When it was time to say goodbye,
she carefully laid her plans.
She didn't shout or curse her lot;
she lovingly took God's hand
(so very different).
She tried to reassure us;
she tried to calm our fears.
So accepting of her fate,
she gently dried our tears
(oh, so different).
So as each day begins anew,

I think about my mother—
her Irish wit, her love, and strength—
she was like no other.
(Yes, she was different.)
She was different, so very special
in her own loving way.
So giving of her time and self.
I'll miss her,
oh, I'll miss her
all my days.

Dad, the Worrier

He worries when we come home late,
watches the clock, paces the floor.
Impatiently, he flips the light,
then checks the clock once more.
A siren blaring in the night
sends him quickly to the car,
in search of one stray wandering lamb;
he is prepared to travel far.
Then in the distant shining light,
he sees the headlights turn our way.
The tensions leave, and he relaxes;
now comes the end of a hectic day.
Back to the house he quickly goes,
hesitating, just one time more
as he stops and listens impatiently
for the key that turns the door.
He worries when we come home late,
watches the clock, paces the floor.
But it doesn't bother me at all,
I just love him all the more.

Time

If time waits for no one,
why do so many people waste
such a precious commodity?
It almost seems your life
is slowly slipping away.
If all you do is sit and impatiently
stamp out another cigarette, walk aimlessly around,
drink that fifth cup of unwanted coffee,
or chatter endlessly about incidental happenings,
you're wasting part of your life.
If there were only some way to save this time
for another day, another week,
or even another year, when time
is truly running out and you want
to hang on for yet another precious moment.

My Way

I lay no claim to glory
nor wear a laurel wreath.
No trophies sit upon my shelf,
nor ribbon I can bequeath.
Though fame and fortune passed me by,
I feel no sorrow or remorse.
My life has been happy, full of love;
I freely followed this course.
For I have found it's not what you do
but rather how you do it.
For God gives each a special gift,
but you, you must pursue it.

I Planned My Future

It seems like only yesterday,
a million dreams or more away.
Excitedly, I planned my future,
not knowing what was in store.
But I knew just what I wanted,
I set my sights so high.
I was determined to do my best,
but opportunity passed me by.
The years flew fast; I know not how
my castles crumbled and fell.
My spirit was trampled in the dust;
my hopes slipped through an endless well.
But still, I kept my faith alive;
despite the obstacles, I did my best.
I am content with the life I made;
my soul withstood the test.

A Patient's Plea

It's Christmastime;
the season's high.
My battle cry:
"Please ... let me die."
All my life,
I've worked and sweated.
Now, I need time
to rest ... and yet ...

They won't let me go
as I so choose.
Why do they feel
it's a battle they lose?

I've got to stop,
get off this ride
that propels me now
until I slide
to a senseless life
of pain and sorrow,
pure torture. I know
I can't face tomorrow.

Please help me Lord.
Oh, hear my plea.
It's time to go.
Please set me free.

It's Christmastime;
the season's high.
My battle cry:
"Please ... let me die."

History Repeated

The woman stopped dead in her tracks and said,
"Oh, dear God, no."
The utter shock, the disbelief.
"I can't believe it's so."
I saw her face. I sensed her grief,
the terror, yes, the strain.
And as I watched, I saw her change
as she recalled the pain
of past events that came alive
within her heart and mind.
She wiped her eyes and tried to speak.
Her voice was soft and kind.
"I dearly love my country."
She slowly looked around. Her tears fell fast and
amid the sorrow, there was not a sound.
"I just do not comprehend or clearly understand
why people do the things they do to desecrate this land."
If men could live and let live and show respect
for all, we'd never have this moment of bitter sorrow and regret.
The violence that has hit again reopens wounds once healed.
History will soon record this time, a chapter best left sealed.
For how can we explain to generations yet unborn,
the violence that plagued us all, leaving many spent and torn.
This is a time of great unrest, insecurity, and fear.
The people react with disbelief to find such violence near.
What can we do, where can we turn, to find the solace we desperately need?
Has God forsaken this foolish world because his words we did not heed?
Please help us, Lord, and show us how to rid the world of sorrow.
Restore our courage, repair our pride so that we may face a new tomorrow.

His Infinite Plan

A foolish man seeks to find
a castle in the sky,
never knowing or aware
that life is passing by.
With great beauty all around him,
he seeks the mountain far,
gazing to the heavens
at the brightest distant star.
Until one day, by chance, perhaps,
he glances to the ground.
Suddenly, he discovers
a secret most profound.
That he spent a lifetime seeking
a treasure rare,
never knowing, little dreaming,
completely unaware.
That life is what you make it.
Yesterday now is past.
Tomorrow is uncertain,
and so, the die is cast.
So live each hour to the fullest.
Enjoy each day you can.
Fond memories come from moments rare,
part of God's amazing plan.

I Felt So Down

I felt so down just yesterday,
the world all dark and dreary.
My heart was heavy, shoulders bent,
my body oh so weary.
I could have cried so easily.
In fact, I did that night.
I wondered why no one noticed.
I felt so bad, so uptight.
I went to bed so burdened,
my pillow damp with tears.
I hugged myself and gently sobbed,
blocking out my fears.

Bewildered

When bewildered and full of sorrow,
afraid to face a dull tomorrow,
rise above the hurting things.
Have faith in God and spread your wings.
Hear the golden voice of love
and know that you can rise above
the earthly trials that come your way.
Love and hope will change your day.

Please, Help Me, Lord

I feel so tired, so depressed.
I don't know what to do.
I thought I'd stop and rest awhile,
share my thoughts with you.

No one seems to notice I'm not
smiling much today.
I'm just downhearted.
There's nothing much to say.

I kinda felt you were a friend
and I could talk to you,
with a shoulder I could lean on,
since I'm feeling sad and blue.

Please, help me, Lord, and see me through
the days that lie ahead.
Give me the strength I need to face
the nights I've come to dread.

Life

We're born.
We live, we love, we die,
and so the story goes,
yet things remain undone,
like a chapter yet untold.
No time to do them, so we say,
soon the years are gone.
Why does time go by so fast?
Can't you see that this is wrong?
Then regret takes hold and lo,
we wonder why.
No matter what, there has to be
time set aside to die.
Why not make the time to do what you want,
when the years before you are long?
Gaze at the blue sky up above,
sit and dream, sing a song.
Why not take the time to do what we can
and not let it pass us by?
Make the most of our brief stay here on earth.
Leave no regret behind.
When it's time to say goodbye.

Unsung Heroes

In times of want and hunger,
all mankind can hear the call.
They rally round, tighten belts,
help out, one and all.

During times of strain or crisis,
human nature digs down deep.
People marvel; they wonder
at such strength, yet I keep
thinking …
The one who has real courage
is the man who day by day.
Faithfully fulfills his duty
in his own simple way.

In truth, these are the heroes
that make our country strong,
solidly lay the foundation,
teaching children right from wrong.

These are the unsung heroes,
the real backbone of our land.
Uncomplainingly, they live their lives,
and with God walk hand in hand.

Maturity

Maturity is the ability to control anger and settle differences
without violence or destruction.

Maturity is patience, the willingness to pass up immediate pleasure
in favor of the long-term gain.

Maturity is perseverance, the ability to sweat out a project or a
situation in spite of opposition and discouraging setbacks.

Maturity is unselfishness, responding to the needs of others,
often at the expense of one's own desires or wishes.

Maturity is the capacity to face unpleasantness and frustration,
discomfort and defeat, without complaint or collapse.

Maturity is humility.

Maturity is being big enough to say, "I was wrong," and when right,
not to say, "I told you so."

Maturity is the ability to make a decision and stand by it.
The immature spend their lives exploring endless possibilities—
then do nothing.

Maturity means dependability, keeping one's word,
coming through in a crisis.

The immature are masters of the alibi, confused and disorganized.
Their lives are a maze of broken promises, former friends, unfinished
business and good intentions, which never materialize.

Maturity is the art of living in peace with that which we cannot change.

The Best For Last

It's great to be back to our class reunion,
amid memories from the past
with the chance to live again,
days we felt would always last.
Together we planned our future dreams.
We saw a few come true.
Despite obstacles along the way,
we made it back to you.
Many years have come and gone.
We've shared many memories
of high school and the senior prom.
Remember how the boys used to tease?
Time hasn't dulled the sweetness,
though the growing years are past.
Seeing all of you here today—
it saved the best for last.

I Called

I don't know why I did it,
being so scared and all.
I felt just like I used to
when I was a kid so small.
I had that funny feeling,
a tingle down my spine.
But I know how much I loved you
and longed to make you mine.
So I bravely called you on the phone.
I remember so well; I felt a chill.
I came right out and said, "I love you,
and I know I always will."
First, you laughed, then you cried.
I really thought I blew it.
Then you said, "I love you too,"
but I really thought you knew it.
Whenever I feel discouraged
or somehow down on life,
I stop and remember how happy we were
the day I asked you to be my wife.
Then all the problems seem so small.
I know we can handle anything,
for you are there beside me,
no matter what the years may bring.

Quiet Interlude

My eyelids are heavy.
I breathe a sigh
as I close out the world
and give way to that inner voice,
softly pulling me down.
Down, to where I do not know.
The noises are dimmer now,
and there's a peaceful warmth
surrounding me.
As I sink deeper and deeper
into some faraway void,
I cannot move nor speak,
just listen to the sounds.
A bell ringing somewhere,
a fan, a magazine with pages
being turned,
water running.
Where are the voices I had heard?

I could feel myself
drifting, drifting,
totally relaxed and completely oblivious
to my surroundings.
Suddenly, my thoughts are interrupted,
and a gentle tugging brings me back.
The voices are now surrounding me again
as I realize,
I had fallen asleep.

Some Folks

Some folks are such a funny lot.
They worry so of what they have not,
with not a thought of life and love,
nor sight to view the sky above.
But oh, the ones who bow their heads
and thank the Lord for daily bread
are richer far and truly blessed;
in simple things find happiness.

Old Age

Old age comes to all in time,
often just when in your prime.
I'll have no regrets; I won't be sad,
I'm grateful for the love I've had.
The laughter and the tears did fall.
Ah, yes, I've had them one and all.
So hold me close and comfort me,
for the best is yet to be.

To Let You Know

If you remember me today, you must
remember too, that I adored you, darling,
and thought the world of you.
You must remember that I said
how it would break my heart if anything should change your mind
and we should ever part.
Well, this is just to let you know
that when you went away, you broke my heart,
and it is still a broken heart today.
I cannot find a smile as sweet as the one you gave to me
or any solace that would match your loving company.
This is just to tell you, dear, wherever you may go,
I still adore and love you more than you will ever know.

Home

Home is the place we argue the most
and are treated the best.
It's where we sing and dance and love,
put patience to the test.

Home is a world of itself,
a place that some forsake.
Each day adds to memories.
All learn to give and take.

Home holds dear all things we love.
It's the center of our affection.
Each brick and stone, piece of wood,
not a palace but to us perfection.

Home is where we always come back to
no matter where we roam.
Our heart will guide us to the path
that eventually brings us home.

I Believe

I believe there is a God
who loves us one and all.
I believe He plans our lives
and answers most every call.

A just and honest being,
who knows the flesh is weak.
He only asks we try our best.
Perfection He does not seek.

When judgment day rolls around,
He'll say, "Now take a look,
your actions during life;
speak more loudly than My Book."

The seeds you've sown, so shall you reap,
and then He'll heave a sigh.
As day by day seems to pass
right before your eye.

I believe there is a God,
who is just and ever fair,
and that He plans our daily lives,
tenderly, with care.

Impatient

I sit and wait for you to come
and grow impatient by the hour.
Yet, if by chance, for some unknown reason,
you would not arrive as planned,
my impatience would dissolve
and concern would take hold.
And I would then pray only for your safe return,
unmindful of the time between.

Your Nurse Weeps for You

I see the tears
flowing uncontrollably
as you absorb the latest report.
You asked them to be honest,
and they were.
But oh, how unprepared
you were to accept
the full truth.
So much to do.
so little time
to do it in.
Your thoughts are scattered
in all directions,
which way to go.
Suddenly, you're
totally overcome
with the realization
that all things,
at some time,
must come to an end.
And at this moment
our eyes are locked
as you realize,
I, too, feel your pain.

A Mother to Her Son

Oh, son of mine, so caught
in the pain of becoming a man.
Please, believe me when I say,
"I want to help you if I can."
You say I don't understand.
You're so unsure and full of fear,
and yet, in truth, our memories
are very, very clear.
As you sit there so overwrought
with hands so clenched and tight.
I want to hold and tell you
the miracle does not happen overnight.
These growing pains are sharp.
Your tears burst forth to join the fight,
so please, my son, be patient
and try to understand.
I'm waiting here to help you
on your journey to becoming a man.

Remember Camelot

A feeling of unfulfillment has settled over the land.
In our hearts, a weight was placed.
Destiny played a hand.
At night my thoughts still wonder
as I try to hide my grief
and mourn that of all men living.
Why was his stay so brief?
Time has passed, life goes on,
and still the people mourn.
The terrible shock has softened some,
but the sadness lingers on.
So briefly did he touch our lives,
so short his journey here.
This father, husband, mother's son,
his memory ever dear.
No matter what was said or felt,
it just was not enough,
the shining knight from Camelot,
his light so swiftly snuffed.

Angel Baby

In heaven, there was an angel,
a perfect angel boy.
He jumped and climbed the moonbeams,
a darling little joy.
He's swing upon a falling star.
Slide down the Milky Way.
His little feet moved so fast,
he fell down every day.
Now this little angel somehow knew
he wasn't like any other.
So, one day, he said to God,
please, sir, I'd like a mother.
Someone to watch me real close
so I won't fall down so much.
Hold me, love me, heal my hurts
with a tender, gentle touch.
And please, God, I'd like a father,
someone big and strong,
to help me learn to be a man,
to teach me right from wrong.
And so, God sent this angel
down to earth one day,
to be part of a special family
to learn, to laugh, to play.
He steals the heart of all he meets.
His smile is like no other.
For God gave him a father strong
and a kind and gentle mother.

Aftermath

'Twas the day after Christmas
and all through the house,
were wrappings and boxes
from each shirt and blouse.
The stockings were flung
on the couch and the chair.
The contents of all were scattered
here and there.
No longer nestled
and snug in their beds,
the children were fighting
and banging their heads.
'Tis true they were angels
the whole week before.
Now they're like devils,
but who's keeping score?
The house was just sparkling
like Mister Clean.
Now it's a disaster,
not a clean spot to be seen.
I've just received word
that before a fortnight,
company is coming, oh woe is me;
I sure would like
to salvage the tree.
When out in the kitchen
there arose a great shout.
Good heavens, I thought,
what's my husband about?
A misplaced nail
had found its way into his shoe.
I couldn't help thinking,
he needs something to do.
As the noise of the day
slowly crept to a roar.
The children (God love them)

fell asleep on the floor.
From the family room couch,
I heard a great snore.
At the same time, the wind
slammed shut the front door.
I found myself yawning and felt a great tear
of joy or bewilderment—I'm really not clear.
But I looked at them all, so precious and dear,
and with some misgivings, I thought of next year.

Waiting

The waiting is the hard part.
At first, you have a cup of coffee,
chat a while, and then
thumb through a magazine.
This becomes very old very quickly
as you start to watch the clock.
The second hand slowly starts its laborious ascent
upward, upward.
In the meantime, you start
to pace the floor, back and forth.
Now you become a people watcher.
The young gentleman,
so calm, yet tense. A middle-aged man
reading a magazine. The heavy-set
woman actually sleeping.
Myself, first calm and accepting, but
as the second hand now starts
the downward descent, becoming more anxious,
nervous, and quite concerned
with what is now a long delay.

My Dad

"Clean your plate," my dad would say,
when all the kids were small.
"Clean your plate," and we all knew
we had to eat it all.

It's funny how the years have flown,
yet things remain the same.
We're all grown up and married
and play the same old game.

"Clean your plate," we tell our kids,
like my dad made us do.
And though he now has gone away,
I find I think of him each day,
and I know my kids do too!

A Prayer for the New Year

Oh, Lord, please let me be strong of mind.
Show love and happiness to all mankind.
Let me always do my best
to make my life worthwhile.
To see good in all I meet,
greet life with a smile.
Let me learn from past mistakes,
do better every day,
be happy, cheerful to all I meet
as I pass along life's way.
Let me live a life worthwhile,
one free from hate and worry.
Let me leave my mark behind,
midlife's hustle and flurry.
Let everyone know I did my best
each day of every year,
and when the new year echos in,
they'll know that I've been here.

Our House

Our house was always just the one
where kids all stopped to play,
"I want to know where my kids are,"
my mother used to say.

Our grass was worn in many spots
and as my mom would say,
"I can't worry about the yard being bare.
It's kids I'm raising today."

We survived the early days,
and no matter what may occur.
I realize now, when I think back,
just how lucky we truly were.

Mom never seemed to mind the mess
or the noise we'd invariably make,
and when I think back, she was always ready
with cookies, milk, and cake.

We all had our chores to do,
each and every day.
Oh the times I felt "put upon"
when I wanted to go out and play.

Holiday Mix-Up

I thought about it all week long,
a day my very own.
I planned so many special things to do.
I could feel the tingle of excitement
as I made my plans, I felt just like I did
when in school.
I would shop—that was for sure—
I had typing I could do,
a book to read, and a letter overdue.
But when the day arrived, the time flew fast away.
All my special plans just went askew.
I did go shopping, but for food,
and I baked a birthday cake,
babysat and did the laundry too.
My special day forgotten, but I'm hopefully, making plans
to do all the things I planned to do,
when the children return to school.

Quiet of the Night

I find strength in the quiet of night
and look for peace within,
when I am weary and so tired
and lack the will to win.
There's something about the quiet
that makes me more aware
that God, in His infinite mercy,
has placed me in his care.

Divorce

I'm not sure what the hardest part really is.
So many years together, and suddenly these years
are condensed to a few boxes, sitting alone
in the corner of the living room.
Oh, how my heart aches as I watch our home
being torn apart, piece by piece.
Questions tumble through my mind.
Is this the answer?
Are we making the right decision?
I need time alone.
Time to heal the hurt and the pain,
time to allow me to think clearly again.
This is so hard. But what about when
we first decided something had to be done?
I think a numbness set in and somehow
cushioned the pain.
Ah, so many years, so many tears.
Please, remember me kindly,
for I truly did love you, and
somewhere, somehow, sometime,
maybe we'll be able to find
that long-lost love once again.

Death

My daughter slowly entered the room,
eyes dry with unshed tears.
"I'm all cried out," she softly said,
and with sadness turned her head
(her voice held hidden fears.)

"I don't understand. It just isn't fair
that God should take my teacher.
Everyone loved her. Doesn't God care?
Oh why, why couldn't she stay?"

I held my daughter gently,
for I knew she loved her teacher so.
I tried to help her understand.
Tenderly I took her hand and said,
"We often do not know."

Why things happen when they do
or why she couldn't stay.
But I know God had a reason,
for everything has a season,
so each day we must pray.

That time will ease the sorrow.
Hope will dull the pain,
for when you think of her each day,
remember, she's just a prayer away,
and one day soon,
you'll meet again.

Slowly my daughter lifted her head.
Her eyes were shining bright.
"I think I know what you mean.
Things may not be what they seem,
but then they turn out right."

I softly said a silent prayer
that God had heard my plea
to somehow make her understand.
She calmly came and took my hand,
and I knew she truly did see.

First Communion Day

Little angels
Dressed in white,
Radiant, smiling faces.

Little cherubs
Bow their heads
And dutifully take their places.

Smiling now,
Eyes aglow,
their halos brightly shining.

They're gently led
to meet their God.
No one knows they're pining

To be off
to their treehouse,
in old pants with patches.

Then they wouldn't
have to try
to hide the cuts and scratches.

Nurses

With God as our head nurse,
an angel as His aid.
Our way to heaven is already paved.
Our scissors for a rosary.
Our watch to set the time.
Our cap will be a passport.
What's left is just the climb.
White shoes will do the roadwork.
Our heart will set the pace.
Our healing hands now at rest.
We'll meet God face to face.

Response to Spring

I really hate to house clean.
It's such a "have-to" thing.
I'd rather watch Mother Nature
prepare a lovely spring.

I had the best intentions.
I ran the sweeper, stripped the bed,
but something called me outside
to watch a squirrel instead.

I know I should have scrubbed the floors.
The windows are a fright,
but spring arrives just once a year
and is such a happy sight.

I'll clean the house tomorrow
or yet another day,
but now I've got to welcome spring
before she slips away.

We Love You, Dear

We know at times
you doubt our love
when we shout and yell.
But it's a habit
parents have,
for we're hesitant to tell
you, we truly, truly
love you, dear.
With all our heart, we care.
We want to help you grow,
expand,
to be kind, to share
your youthfulness,
your vibrancy,
your honesty, your soul
with those you meet
along life's way.
But, above all, to let you know
the world would be
a sorry place
without a child's love.
So even though we seldom say it,
we thank the Lord above
for every moment, every hour
we spend each day with you.
And God willing.
You know our love
is honest and ever true.

A Mother's Lament

Peace and quiet, I dearly love,
with the house sparklingly clean.
But with a houseful of little ones,
such perfection is only a dream.

A lady of leisure with time to relax,
write a letter, or read.
Even this is hard to arrange
when someone starts to bleed.

A place for everything sounds great indeed,
with everything in its place.
To be known as the perfect hostess—what's that?
Jelly smeared on my face?

A Gentle Touch

How do you let someone know the way
you feel without telling them so?

What do you do to put their minds at rest
or let them know you love them best?

Maybe an outstretched hand will tell someone
special just where you stand.

A gentle touch to let them know how much
you care without telling them so.

So, I'll touch you gently. I won't say a word.
My beating heart, I'm sure, will be heard.

My touch, as soft as the morning dew,
will tell your soul how I love you.

The Seasons

I really hate the winter.
There's nothing much to do.
I hate going to work in the morning
like I hated going to school.
I guess I get kinda lonesome
when the roads are too bad to drive.
I feel so cooped up and alone,
almost more dead than alive.
I really can't wait for summer,
to go for a stroll each night,
to feel the soft cool breezes blow,
to watch a bird in flight,
to walk to the corner for ice cream
even take a cool-off ride,
meeting neighbors coming and going,
enjoying the great outside.

To My Daughter

What you throw is what you sow,
I've told that daughter mine,
referring, of course, to the clothes
she's asked to hang out on the line.
It's like she really doesn't know
pins are made to hang the clothes,
and I get so tired of yelling,
as every good mother knows.
The strangest figures do appear
as if from outer space,
An upside-down, inside-out shirt
takes on a strange-looking face.
Her father's socks are all askew.
They're thrown this way and that.
I often take a second look.
I thought they were a bat.
But the strangest-looking article
I've yet found on the line
Is the pant with one leg
Thrown over a clump
that turned out to be a dress of mine.

The Window Pane

Remember when you were just a child
and couldn't go out to play
but had to stay in the house;
it was such a cold, wet day?

There was nothing much to do
but sit and watch the rain
or draw a small child's picture
on the steamed-up windowpane.

I thought my mom would make a fuss
with the window smeared and all,
but she smiled gently, and I somehow knew,
she was remembering when she was small.

Oh, I remember feeling so proud
the day I wrote my name,
when I was just a little child,
on the steamed-up windowpane.

A Prayer at the End of the Day

Oh Lord, I sit here tired and worn.
It's been a busy day,
with the rush, the hustle, and the bustle
that often comes my way.
It's not that I'm complaining, Lord.
Just feeling a little strained.
I guess unappreciated,
and that gives me pain.
Sometimes, no matter what I do,
I never get ahead.
I get so frustrated, so upset.
The days I truly dread.
I guess I should be thankful, Lord,
I've made it through this day.
Also, be glad I'm healthy, Lord
What more can I really say?
Except I'm glad You're listening.
I needed someone to share
the heaviness that's in my heart.
I guess, someone to care.
So, thank you, Lord, for listening.
I feel better, more relaxed.
As long as you're here to give me strength,
That's really all I ask.

A Special Time

There's a quiet moment of each day
from dusk to early dawn,
where I have found a restful peace.
Hurry, times are gone.

The hustle and the bustle
have quieted and settled some,
and in this special moment
the heavens seem to hum.

This is the time to just relax,
unshackle chains that bind,
explore the heavens, venture forth
with a free and open mind.

For God has given freely
far horizons to explore,
and in this peaceful time of day,
he opens the magic door.

When I'm Gone

I want to write for the ones I love,
my family, my friends, the people I know.
I want to remember each minute, each hour
I spent on earth,
I love it so.
I want to record, by the power of the pen,
each precious day, of every year,
to let them know how important they were,
how glad I was to be here.
And when I am gone, I ask but one thing:
they think of me kindly each day.
And if time permit, God grant it be so,
they read what I had to say.

The Secret of Life

Don't be discouraged or saddened,
when a chapter in life does end.
Just realize you've come to a crossing
in the road—a little bend.
You must have faith in the morrow,
when your work years are behind,
for only the one who has a stout heart,
a place in the future will find.
You don't have to spend a fortune
to find your pot of gold.
Just open your heart and be aware
of what the future can hold.
For the secret of life is to look ahead,
be happy just to be.
Enjoy each day to the fullest.
Be thankful you're alive and free.

Happiness

Sometimes it takes great effort
to find happiness, 'tis true,
and I find that keeping it
seems difficult to do.
Some people think that happiness
is for those in places high,
who have great wealth and even fame.
They let it slip right by.
Happiness lies within the reach
of those who give a part
of their time and of themselves,
directly from the heart.
For like the smile you give away
to each man and his brother.
It returns to you a hundredfold
so you may give it to another.

"Diet—a Matter of Mind over Platter"

It's not much fun to do without.
Your stomach is so tied up in knots.
You want all the food you happen to see.
Despite what you have, you crave the have-nots.

Your day is filled with cottage cheese,
self-restraint, and exercise.
Your nights are filled with fantasies,
chocolate sundaes and cherry pies.

Yet there is one consolation
as your daily struggle grows.
You now can do things you haven't done for years,
like reaching that top shelf or touching your toes.

So take heart, ladies everywhere.
Your future goal you will not shatter.
Just do your best, and remember each day,
"Diet is a matter of mind over platter."

Why Me?

I lie here, staring at four walls.
I watch the drip, drip, drip
of my intravenous solution,
slowly flow through the
transparent tubing
into my veins,
into my body.
My eyes burn with tears now dry.
I hear muffled voices outside my door
and a shrill siren
in the background.
Why am I so aware of all these living sounds,
now that I'm so near the end and about
to travel a road I've never been before?
And never wanted to see.
Where is all the peace and acceptance
I'm supposed to feel at such a time?
All I know is this churning
in the pit of my stomach
won't go away,
and the blinding rage
I feel within makes me
want to scream and ask,
"Why me?"

Smiling Tears

(A Friend's Unexpected Death)

What a waste, I said to myself
as I put down the phone,
shook my head, walked away.
I felt so desolate, so alone.
I thought of many little things
that I never think about.
The grass seemed greener, the air so clear.
I wanted to scream; I wanted to shout.
I thought of all the fun times
that he would never know—
a warm summer's day, the football games,
that first winter's snow.
I remembered all the plans he had,
his future hopes, his dreams.
I closed my eyes, heard his unsung songs.
How very unfair life seems.
Oh, dear God, what a waste it is.
I'll remember his smile for years.
The funny little jokes he told
have me smiling through my tears.

Who Rocks the Cradle?

When God sends mothers to earth each day,
He is heard to softly say,
"Into a special role you're hurled,
for you have the greatest task in the world."

The molding of a human life.
Such a challenge, it's worth all the strife.
You mothers with your gentle hand
have the power to rule the land.

So take this small one entrusted to you.
Raise him to be honest, good, and true.
Show him what's right, do the best you can.
Teach him, love him, make him a man.

Then to the world present him with pride.
No matter the outcome, the best was tried.
This then will be your flag unfurled,
"Who rocks the cradle does rule the world."

Please Remember September

In honor of the firemen who gave their lives September 11, 2001

So brave they were, so unafraid.
They climbed the stairway to heaven, and history was made.
Into the burning building they raced with speed
to carry, to comfort, to fill any need.

On this day of beauty with the air so clear.
It suddenly changed and filled us with great fear.
Giant planes were forced to fly
into twin towers, and many would die.

These brave men came to answer the call.
They gave love, not hate.
They gave their all.

History will note and mark their deed,
their gift to the country in this time of need.

They gave up their hopes, their dreams, to unite
all Americans together so we'd stand up and fight
for this country we love, this freedom so dear,
and never forget the brave men who died here.

So Americans please, forever remember
this day of terror that came in September.

The Housewife's Prayer

Dear Lord, please help me through the day.
There is so much to do.
Cooking, cleaning, scrubbing,
Baking cookies today for school.

I sometimes think that no one cares.
Not true, I guess, and yet,
I feel so tired, really worn.
I guess they just forget.

I really don't need special things
or want a great reward,
just to know they appreciate me
and love me—that's all, Lord.

Maybe a thank-you, or a smile,
a hug at the end of the day.
It'd sure brighten my spirit,
even chase my blues away.

Vinegar and Wine

Life is a mixture of vinegar and wine,
and if you stop you'll see.
When you take a close, close look,
that's how it's meant to be.

This drama of life is exciting,
meeting with people each day.
But if nothing new ever happened,
you'd be discouraged in every way.

If today is beautiful, fulfilling.
Enjoy it the best you know how.
There's no guarantee how long it will last,
so treasure the here and now.

Into each life, some rain must fall
onto God's grass and earth.
But only a challenge that's met head-on
can strengthen and double life's worth.

So if sweet wine begins to turn
and trouble comes your way.
Just remember, vinegar adds spice to life.
A challenge to be met each day.

One added thought I'd like to share,
the combination, sweet 'n' sour, is so fine.
When the rain leaves, the sun will shine.

Dear Dad

I find it hard to realize
you're left your earthly home.
We wait in daily expectation,
thinking you may phone.

Mom doesn't believe you've gone away.
The house seems empty and bare.
She tries to fill her days
but somehow doesn't care.

I know you had a good life,
one full of love and all.
I'm certain you were ready to go,
maybe waiting the call.

But, there's an empty feeling
I just can not explain.
We visit Mom and know
we won't see you again.

I hope you're watching over us
in your special way,
because the years go quickly
each and every day.

We'll have a big reunion
where we all will be
together again as before,
the whole family.

Autumn

Autumn is a golden sunset
with bittersweet and burning leaves.
A sudden splash of color by
some unknown artist, brightening
the forests and roadways.
Or a marshmallow roast by a huge bonfire,
welcoming in the football season.
Children returning to school,
ripened grain pleading to be harvested,
walking through mountains of fallen leaves
and crushing them beneath your feet.
Indian summer, Halloween, and pumpkins.
Autumn is a crispy coolness in the air,
when a gentle breeze captures the last leaf,
and, against all odds, attempts
to return it to from whence it came,
in vain.
Autumn is a peaceful quiet,
where tranquility will reign.

The Lord's Guidance

I find as time has moved along,
dreams mellowed with the years.
For every lost hope on the way,
I've shed a million tears.
Still, I falter and grow afraid.
There's so much left to do.
The future looks so bleak and gray.
Who will help me, who?
Who will share my lonely path,
offer a helping hand?
Suddenly a bright light shone through the night
to help me understand
that with God's help I shall find
peace and love, above all hope,
and His guidance to find
the tools to cope.

My Treasure Chest

My treasure chest of memories
is opened every year.
Always at Thanksgiving time,
do thoughts begin to stir.
I think about my family,
the abundance of kilt and kin,
a giant turkey on the table
and neighbors dropping in.
I remember we always bowed our heads,
and with a prayerful nod,
gratefully acknowledged
these blessings from our God.
The women chattered, children played.
The men all watched the game.
We sat and talked into the night
and were so glad they came.
I'm thankful for these memories,
for truly I am blessed
with happiness that never fades
but overflows my treasure chest.

The Wish

When he was just a small boy,
he wished he'd grow up and be
like his big brother in school
(one of the big guys).

When he was in school,
he hated it and wished
he was old enough to quit
(one of the tough guys).

When he was fifteen,
he felt no one
could teach him anymore,
so he did just that
(cynicism grew as the years passed).

When he was twenty-five
and out of a job,
he wished he was older
And out of the rat race
(he found no peace).

When he was older and unable to work,
there was nothing to do
but seek oblivion.
His wish was granted
(one last time).

Trust In God

I believe in motherhood,
America, and apple pie.
I believe in freedom
and for it would gladly die.
I believe in God and heaven above.
I believe in marriage
and in love.
I believe in living
and letting live.
I believe in faith and trust,
and I make allowances if I must.
I try to be forgiving
in every way I can
and do my part to aid
in the infinite plan.
I have known sorrow and real joy,
from the death of a loved one
to the birth of my baby boy.
Disappointments don't upset me,
for I have found, you see,
that our Heavenly Father hears every call
and somehow, miraculously, answers them all.

Embered Ashes

As the flames darted in and out
between the logs.
They cast a warming glow
across the empty room.
They danced and leaped
in ecstatic radiance,
their many colors shooting arrows
of brightness into the night.
But, once consumed by the grasping fingers
of the flames, the logs
disintegrated before my very eyes.
The lovely brilliance dwindled, and
only with great effort now
could a few sparks be seen.
For a fleeting moment,
I thought of life and death and
how like a burning log it is.
Reaching, seeking, making its presence known.
Then, when it reaches the very heights
of perfection, it starts the downward trek,
toward the embered ashes of the unknown.

The Ocean

There is no beginning, no obvious end,
to the gentle water flowing to and fro.
The heavens seem to step down
as though to meet a friend,
merging softly with the beauty of the flow.

This symphony continues as the tide dances high,
softly touching the star-studded night.
The Master adds this gentle touch,
contentedly breathes a sigh,
as He sprinkles soft fluffs of angel white.

No Desperate Need

I never knew how simple love could be.
A feeling of contentment, like a quiet, tranquil sea.

I used to think it meant excitement and desire.
A feeling of unrest, a burning fire.

But now I understand, and things are clear.
There is no desperate need when love is near.

Faith, Hope, and Love

Have Faith,
for Faith forms the future.

Take Hope,
for without Hope, there is no tomorrow.

Give Love,
for Love is what makes life worth living.

One Little Child

It's amazing how one little child
can liven up each day.
He's the center of all attention
with his sweet and gentle way.
It's really quite surprising,
one so little can mean so much.
And wonder of wonders I have found
pure magic in his gentle touch.
There's nothing like a brand-new babe
to spread happiness and good cheer.
There's a special feeling all around
since little John did appear.

Time for a Change

I needed to take one last look
before I said goodbye.
Fondly, I walked around the room,
then softly began to cry.
It really hurt to see again
what had once been part of me.
Regrets set in for all I'd lost,
the life that used to be.
It's strange how pathways
twist and bend,
how dreams shatter and die,
I needed to take one last look
before I said goodbye.

An Open Heart

There is beauty in every day
and everywhere you go.
Just take a closer look to prove
that what I say is so.

There's beauty in a budding rose,
the satin grass so green.
The sunrise glistening in the early morn,
the prettiest ever seen.

The sunset in the evening,
the rainbow after a storm.
A sleeping babe held snuggly safe
by his mother, to keep him warm.

There's beauty all around us
wherever we chance to be.
But only one who opens his heart
to life can truly see.

Nothing Seems the Same

Nothing seems to be the same.
It's all so different now.
You barely ever speak my name.
Have you forgotten how?

Everything now seems so strained
as tempers daily fly.
My heart is heavy, ever pained.
Days just drag on by.

What is the answer, where do I look?
How do I know what is wrong?
No longer peaceful, it's like someone took
the melody out of our song.

End: Chapter One

As I watched my youngest climb aboard
the school bus that first day.

His farewell wave was happy and his
smile so bright and gay.

But I felt a twinge within my heart,
like an arrow had pierced the sun.

Sadly, I turned back to the house
and thought, "End: Chapter One!"

Bridge of Love

A generation gap is nothing more
than misunderstanding
between young and not so young.

Just as two islands are connected with a bridge,
two generations can be connected
with the bridge of love.

To You, My Love

I give you my heart to have and hold
every minute of the day.
I give you my love, strong and bold.
The years can't change or sway.

I give you my soul, a spirit free,
I give you all there is of me.
I pray that we will never part.
To you, my love, I give my heart.

Another Year

I can't believe another year
has somehow slipped on by.
At times I'm not really sure
if we should laugh or cry.
But nonetheless
it's been great fun,
walking through this busy life.
I just can't believe
it's been so long
since I became your wife.
So, happy anniversary.
We've had such fun together,
and hopefully the days ahead
will continue with fair weather.

Awakening

As I sat in church this morning,
with the people all around,
at once, the meaning of it all
seemed suddenly to astound.
To think the teachings of a single man
led us here to pray,
to unite all people in the world,
to make them one someday.
Dear Lord above, please help us,
with Your goodness and Your might.
Find a way for peace on earth
to all mankind; please shed Your light.

An Angel Named Karen

There once was an angel named Karen
whom God sent to earth one day.
His message was clear as he whispered,
"My dear, it will be a very short stay."

God poked around the moonbeams
to find the perfect pair,
and smilingly told Karen
He would place her in their care.

A sacred trust He gave them,
for indeed it was quite rare
for earthlings to raise an angel,
one so young and fair.

Karen loved her newfound home,
and her newfound family too.
She laughed and played and had great fun
and my, she really grew.

She learned to bake, she learned to mend,
she even went to school.
She learned to read, had a best friend,
and followed the golden rule.

But then one day she had a dream,
when she was only ten,
and there was God calling her
to come back home again.

So Karen left her earthly home
so precious and so dear,
and as she softly slipped away,
there fell one tiny tear.

And now, at night, I watch the sky
and look both near and far,
for somewhere in the heavens,
there's a bright new shining star.

Reach for the Sky

He gave up a dream
to show his love,
turned his life around.
Aimed for the heavens
and found the stars
were closer
to the ground.
His hopes were filed
in his heart.
Never would they die.
Someday soon,
he'd try again
to reach, reach for the sky.

The Dentist

If it were within my power,
I'd send a proclamation
that would outlaw tooth decay in every land and nation.
I'd take the drills, the polisher, and yes, the dental floss.
I'd throw them all so far away.
They'd be forever lost.
Then I'd have the dentist be the guard both night and day,
to make sure old tooth decay would never again come this way.

For Andy

He loved most men
and was a friend to all.
His life's battle ended
when he heard the Lord's call.
Please don't feel sorrow that
his life has passed,
for he "lived every moment,
from the first to the very last."
His family and friends
were steadfast to the end.
They loved him dearly,
this brother, son, and friend.
We'll travel more slowly,
so when our chapter closes,
we can honestly say
we too smelled the roses.

I've Learned to Be Me!

Yes, I've suffered, and I know,
how the pain racks and
sears your soul.

Like you, I've stumbled,
wept bitter tears,
cursed the darkness
as I struggled through the years.

But having known defeat,
it's made me stand up straight.
I've grown in strength;
injustice I hate.

My heart is full of love,
my spirit free;
despite all my sufferings,
I've learned to be *me*!

Gossip

"I hate Mondays"
is what she said,
then took a gun
and shot them dead.
Sure a shame
poor mixed-up kid.
She'll burn in hell
for what she did.
Who'd ever figure
she had it in 'er.
Can't blame folks
for being agin' 'er.
How tongues do wag
and heads do turn.
"What'd she get?
Bet she'll burn."
Eight of 'em wounded.
Two are dead.
Wonder what went on
in her head.
"I hate Mondays"
is what she said.
Guess that's why
She shot 'em dead.

My Husband

A restless fifty-year-old man, impatient, a perfectionist.
Self-contained, needing few friends, close to family,
yet a loner with varying moods.
Strong principles, religious, a strict disciplinarian
but fair, honest, hardworking, proud, gentle, and loving.
Have you ever been asked to describe your husband?
Think about it!

Sleep, My Love

I awoke early this morning and let you sleep
because I love to watch your tousled hair and
your near-boyish face at peace. Seems strange
that when you're relaxed; you look so youthful, not fifty.
Maybe because your guard is down, as it
sometimes is when we're together and you
do not have to pretend to be all-wise, all-
knowing. My fingers gently smooth out the
wrinkles on your face, which are no longer
there. Sleep gently, my love, and forgive
me for spying on you at such a defenseless time.

The Gift

I took great pains
and looked around
to find the perfect toy.
I somehow felt I knew
what would please a tiny boy.
A fluffy dog with floppy ears,
a wind-up wagging tail.
I knew it'd make him happy,
bring a smile
without fail.
The paper was very special,
with airplanes, balloons, and colored blocks,
but when he hastily
opened it up,
he played all day with the box.

The Gift of Life

Life is a gift to be cherished.
Each day brings the birth of new hope.
Trust in the future gives courage,
God gives us the strength to cope.
So live your life to the fullest.
Be thankful each hour, every day.
Savor the precious moments
before they slip away.

From Mom

A child who is loved
is loving.
A child independent
is free.
A child who makes someone happy
is a child who was meant to be.
My daughters are such children,
loved, independent, and free,
and make all they meet very happy,
but the proudest of all
is me.

The Rainbow's End

Once, when very young,
I saw a rainbow in the sky.
It didn't seem too far away,
just close as a bird could fly.
So off I went by myself
to search for the pot of gold.
Just over the very next hill at the end
or so I had been told.
But I couldn't seem to find
that rainbow in the sky.
Like magic, it seemed to move away
, or did it climb up high?
I found something much better.
At least, I think I did.
I found the squirrels hiding their nuts
in a tree stump with a lid.
I saw the wild deer running fast.
I knew the pretty woods I found
were just the place for me to be.

The Shroud

Right there on the corner,
I remember it so very well,
the family farm that stood so proud.
Just thinking makes my heart swell.

The children ran the vegetable stand
by the side of the quiet road.
It was fun to pick and weigh the apples
and take pride in what we sold.

But now, when we pass by this place
we loved so well,
it's a vacant lot with weeds overgrown,
and no one can really tell

That on the corner a few years back,
a thriving farm stood proud.
Now weeds and thistles have taken hold,
and time covers it like a shroud.

Danny at Camp

My youngest left for camp today,
his first time away from home.
All smiles, so anxious, full of pep,
ready to fly, ready to roam.
A few days pass, the house so quiet.
A plaintive voice calls on the phone.
"Hi, Mom. Hi, Dad. Everything's fine.
How are things at home?"
A quick rundown of the past few days.
He seemed homesick, I could tell,
but he kept talking cheerful, like
reassuring that all was well.
"I'll call back in a few days more
to make sure you're all okay,"
and as I hung up the phone,
I brushed a tear away.

A Summer's Day

"Oh, I'm fine," the waitress said,
brushing the hair from her moist forehead.
The day was hot and muggy-like.
No one would ever sleep tonight.

I looked around the busy place,
carefully studied each weary face.
The tired housewife looked ready to drop.
A brief reprieve—that's why she stopped.

The farmer with his weathered brow
seemed perplexed with the here and now.
The businessman, all starched and straight.
Such a scowl; his job he must hate.

I couldn't help wonder, and who's to say?
Was there anything special about this hot day?
When around the corner came two little tots,
counting their pennies, their haves and have-nots.

The carefully laid each one on the shelf,
proudly saying, "We cut Mrs. Jones grass and
decided we'd use it all for a treat."

The tot's grin was so big it brightened the room.
Everyone smiled, dispelling the gloom.
The people were happy, not like before.
Still smiling, we all watched them walk out the door.

Old Friends

I ran into an old friend
last week in my hometown
It's strange how some things stay the same.
She's still a character and a clown.

We talked about our high-school years,
junior high and grade school too.
Into the night we reminisced.
The evening really flew.

It seemed we were putting together
a giant puzzle on the floor.
We each remembered a tiny piece,
then searched around for more.

Show Us the Way

The thread that hangs
between life and death
is too fragile to even see,
yet it's held in balance
for both you and me.

No one knows when it may break
as the pendulum swings too far,
but pay you heed when the thread wears
thin with who and where you are.

For life is short, though days seem long,
and each step we take has been said
to shorten our mortal days on earth
and leads to the land of the dead.

Although this seems final and may make us sad,
take heart and remember today,
Our Heavenly Father will be waiting for us
and will lovingly show us the way.

What Is Christmas?

It's a time of love and happiness;
the whole world is sharing.
It's good fellowship and friendship,
both loving and caring.

It's the warmth and closeness
when people are meeting,
that adds the sparkle
to their holiday greeting.
It's the love that comes
with each gift we receive,
but most of all, it's because
we believe.

Breakfast with Santa

Breakfast with Santa, what a treat,
hearing the patter of little feet.
Eyes shining brightly, the air aglow
excitement rising, winter winds blow.
We started out early, we couldn't wait,
scurried along so we wouldn't be late.
The first sight we saw, as we entered the door,
was Santa and Rudolph, and bright lights galore.
The tree was gigantic, all sparkling and bright.
The children sat wide-eyed and took in the sight.
The nutcracker (so big) was a sight to remember,
on this happy day, the thirteenth of December.
Little John was entranced with the songs and the skit.
His eyes seemed to sparkle as the big tree was lit.
Jolly old Santa kept the children a-tingle,
as back and forth between chairs he did mingle.
We sang Christmas songs; we laughed and were gay.
I couldn't help thinking, *What a beautiful way
to start the season with Santa—an idea really neat.*

Contrast

There's a noticeable difference in Bethlehem
since that day so long ago,
when the Christ child first appeared to man
with a certain kind of glow.
Now soldiers line the streets of the town
where Jesus played as a boy.
Their rifles and boots seem to mock and deride
Christ's teaching of goodness and joy.
If suddenly he appeared today,
He would be sad and frown.
Shoulders would droop, eyes would blur,
His hurt would be profound.
"Dear Father," He prayed, "please help them to know,
love and peace is all that we need.
Please open their hearts,
so they'll hear My words,
and My message all will heed."

Valentine

There's been so much of love and stuff;
there's nothin' left to say.
Hope what I done made up ain't bad,
since it's my only way.
I want you for my Valentine,
just mine alone to be,
'cause of all the fish a swimmin' 'round,
you're the only one for me.

I Tried

I've tried and tried as best I could
to write a little poem that would,
with all sincereness and no delay,
bring joy and gladness on Christmas Day.
But try as I would, not a line could I write;
I fumed and fretted all through the night.
It seemed all poems of Christmas Day
were written in every style and way.
So I changed my mind and thought I'd write
nary a line of that Christmas night
when the Christ child came in all his glory
and gave us the very first Christmas story.
But simply say, as best I could,
"Merry Christmas to all, and do be good."

My Loved Ones

I feel I've been richly blessed
my life, my love, my happiness.
My days are full, my life complete.
I pray the Lord each day to keep
my loved ones ever in His sight.
Guide them through each day, each night,
and guide them should they chance to stray.
Back to You, Lord, this I pray.

Busy

He works so hard, day after day.
He never stops; it's just his way.
Trims and weeds, then cuts the grass,
sprays the roses—so many tasks.
Waters the strawberries, tackles more weeds,
paints the furniture, picks the peas.
Why, oh why, does he work that way,
from early dawn 'til his time to pray?

The Empty House

High on a hill for all to see
stands a house that used to be.
Windows shattered, doors boarded;
no sight at all of life once hoarded.

It seems so lonesome, quiet, and still,
a sentry waiting, its rooms to fill.
Memories creep down lonely halls;
a phantom voice softly calls.

If it could speak, what would it say?
Would it dream and hope for yesterday?
Forlorn, forgotten, it stands so proud,
ever waiting with time a shroud.

A Child Prays

I can hear angel wings flutter
when my small one kneels to pray.
Her words are full of trust and hope
as she talks to her God.
I feel as though I am standing
at the doorstep to heaven.
Her innocence and sweetness
restore my faith in the world.
I feel the hope of the future is guaranteed
by the confidence of the young.

In His Sight

No matter how dark the night may be
or how deep the shadows go,
a loving Father watches over us,
surrounds us with His glow.

Although our days seem saddened,
sorrow fills our nights.
Remember Our Loving Father,
who keeps us in His sight.

A Poet

One day, when I was feeling blue,
I asked my God, "What should I do?"
It seemed, despite my busy life
of homemaker, mother, nurse, and wife,
I felt a need to do much more.
Yet, I knew not what was in store.
So, I took my pen in hand,
and, guided by God's loving hand,
I began to write poetry, in hopes to share
my thoughts and dreams and show I care.

Travel to the Top

Consider the world a hill, lad,
and climb it with glory and pride.
The trials and sufferings as steps, lad,
and sorrow as kin to the ride.

The way is hard and slow, lad;
the time it takes is long.
But with God's help and prayers, lad,
we'll travel that hill with a song.

We'll sail over misery and heartache, lad,
and fly around the grief.
We'll ask the saints in heaven, lad,
to give help and strengthen our belief.

After we've traveled that hill, lad,
we'll stop a while and wait.
For we've made our way to the top, lad;
we're now near the golden gate.

Take the Time

Walk a little slower
as you travel on your way,
for the memories of tomorrow
come from what you do and say.

Take a minute longer
before answering sharp and fast,
for once the moment leaves you,
it's then lost and past.

Take time to answer, little ones,
just a minute of the day,
for the memories of tomorrow
come from what you do and say.

The years go by so quickly;
don't let impatience in.
Take time to smell the flowers;
your fellow man befriend.

Walk a little slower
as you travel on your way,
for the memories of tomorrow
come from what you do and say.

The Writer

I think a poet looks beyond
what mortal eyes do see
and somehow finds the secret
of what life is meant to be.

Like looking past the clouds
that appear in the sky,
seeking out the blueness
that may have passed on by.

He contemplates on why things are
or how they chanced to be.
He marvels at God's handiwork;
that's here for all to see.

A poet seems at times endowed
with a seeking, searching mind
and never stops until he knows
his thoughts reach all mankind.

Printed in the United States
By Bookmasters